Guide For Women With ADHD

:

Strategies For Women With Attention Deficit Hyperactivity Disorder To Find Focus And Fulfillment

Introduction

In the realm of attention deficit hyperactivity disorder (ADHD), the experiences of women have often been overlooked or misunderstood. Amidst the complexities of modern life, women with ADHD navigate a unique set of challenges that impact their ability to find focus, fulfillment, and balance. This book, "Guide for Women with ADHD: Strategies for Women with Attention Deficit Hyperactivity Disorder to Find Focus and Fulfillment," is a beacon of support and empowerment tailored specifically for women living with ADHD. Through a lens of understanding and empathy, this guide aims to illuminate the intricacies of ADHD in women and provide practical strategies to help them thrive in various facets of life.

As we delve into the pages of this book, it becomes evident that ADHD manifests differently in women compared to men. Women with ADHD often grapple with internalized struggles, societal expectations, and cultural norms that complicate their journey towards self-discovery and fulfillment. Dispelling myths and stereotypes surrounding ADHD in women is the first step towards fostering a supportive and inclusive environment where women feel empowered to embrace their unique neurodiversity.

Recognizing the importance of diagnosis and seeking professional support is paramount in the journey towards managing ADHD effectively. By understanding their diagnosis and accessing appropriate resources, women with ADHD can embark on a path of self-awareness, growth, and resilience. Moreover, celebrating the strengths inherent in women with ADHD is crucial in reshaping the narrative around the condition. From creativity and intuition to adaptability and empathy, women with ADHD possess a myriad of strengths that contribute to their unique perspectives and contributions to the world.

Navigating challenges without self-judgment is a central theme woven throughout this guide.

Women with ADHD often face internalized stigma and self-doubt, which can hinder their ability to recognize their own worth and potential. By embracing self-compassion and resilience, women can learn to navigate life's obstacles with grace and determination, cultivating a sense of empowerment and agency in their journey.

We are living in a world that constantly demands attention, women with Attention Deficit Hyperactivity Disorder (ADHD) often find themselves navigating a unique set of challenges. "Unleashing Brilliance: A Guide for Women with ADHD" is a comprehensive handbook designed to empower and support women as they embrace their distinctive strengths and navigate the journey towards focus and fulfillment.

There are Strategies for Women with Attention Deficit Hyperactivity Disorder to Find Focus and Fulfillment." Within the intricate landscape of ADHD, the experiences and challenges unique to women have often remained overlooked. This comprehensive guide is designed specifically to address the needs and concerns of women living with ADHD, offering invaluable insights and practical strategies to help them navigate the complexities of daily life with confidence and resilience.

As we embark on this journey together, it is essential to acknowledge the distinct manifestations of ADHD in women. Often overshadowed by stereotypical perceptions and misconceptions, the experiences of women with ADHD differ significantly from those of their male counterparts. By understanding the nuanced aspects of ADHD in women, we can create a more inclusive and supportive environment where women feel empowered to embrace their neurodiversity and harness their strengths.

Diagnosis and seeking professional support are fundamental steps on the path towards managing ADHD effectively. By recognizing the signs and symptoms of ADHD and accessing appropriate resources and interventions, women can gain invaluable insights into their condition and develop personalized strategies for coping and thriving. Through collaboration with healthcare professionals and mental health experts, women can unlock a wealth of tools and resources to support their journey towards wellness and fulfillment.

Central to this guide is the celebration of the unique strengths and abilities inherent in women with ADHD. From creativity and intuition to adaptability and empathy, women possess a rich tapestry of qualities that enrich their lives and the lives of those around them. By embracing and harnessing these strengths, women can cultivate resilience, confidence, and a sense of purpose in their daily endeavors.

Navigating the challenges of ADHD without self-judgment is a key theme explored in this guide. Women often grapple with internalized stigma and feelings of inadequacy, which can hinder their ability to reach their full potential. Through the practice of self-compassion and mindfulness, women can cultivate a deeper sense of self-awareness, acceptance, and inner peace amidst life's complexities.

Effective time management, organization, and self-care strategies are essential components of a balanced and fulfilling life for women with ADHD. By developing practical routines, creating supportive environments, and prioritizing self-care practices, women can enhance their ability to find focus, manage stress, and cultivate emotional well-being.

Throughout this guide, we will explore a wealth of practical tips, techniques, and strategies tailored specifically to the unique needs and challenges of women with ADHD. By embracing a proactive and holistic approach to wellness, women can embark on a journey of self-discovery, growth, and fulfillment. Together, let us navigate the beautiful complexities of life

with ADHD and empower women to find focus
and fulfillment in every aspect of their lives.

Table Of Contents

Chapter 1: Understanding ADHD in Women

- **Dispelling myths and stereotypes**

- **Recognizing the unique manifestations of ADHD in women**
- **The importance of diagnosis and seeking professional support**

<u>Dispelling myths and stereotypes</u>

In the realm of Attention Deficit Hyperactivity Disorder (ADHD), women often find themselves overlooked, misunderstood, and misdiagnosed. For far too long, the popular image of ADHD has been associated with hyperactive boys bouncing off the walls of classrooms. However, the reality is far more nuanced, particularly for women with ADHD.

In this chapter, we embark on a journey to dispel the myths and stereotypes surrounding women and ADHD. We delve into the pervasive misconceptions that have obscured the experiences of countless women, preventing them from seeking the support and understanding they deserve.

Myth 1: ADHD Only Affects Boys: One of the most enduring myths about ADHD is that it predominantly affects boys. Historically, research and diagnostic criteria have been based on male-centric symptoms, leading to the underdiagnosis and misdiagnosis of girls and women. The truth is that ADHD manifests differently in females, often presenting as inattentiveness rather than hyperactivity.

Myth 2: ADHD Is Just a Childhood Disorder: Another misconception is that ADHD is a condition that children outgrow as they mature into adulthood. While symptoms may change over time, ADHD can persist well into adulthood, affecting women in various aspects of their lives, including education, career, relationships, and self-esteem.

Myth 3: Women With ADHD Are Lazy or Unmotivated: Women with ADHD often face unfair judgments of laziness or lack of motivation due to their difficulties with focus, organization, and time management. These misconceptions fail to recognize the neurological differences that underlie ADHD and undermine the immense effort that women with ADHD exert to navigate daily challenges.

Myth 4: ADHD Is Just a Lack of Discipline or Willpower: Another harmful stereotype suggests that ADHD is simply a matter of discipline or willpower. However, ADHD is a neurodevelopmental disorder characterized by differences in brain structure and function, affecting executive functions such as impulse control, attention, and working memory. Women with ADHD possess immense strengths and talents that may be overshadowed by societal expectations and stigma.

Myth 5: Women With ADHD Cannot Succeed or Thrive: Perhaps the most damaging myth is the belief that women with ADHD cannot succeed or thrive in life. Nothing could be further from the truth. With the right support, strategies, and self-compassion, women with

ADHD can unlock their potential, pursue their passions, and lead fulfilling lives rich in accomplishment and meaning.

By confronting these myths and stereotypes head-on, we pave the way for a deeper understanding of ADHD in women and empower women to embrace their unique neurodiversity. In the chapters that follow, we will explore practical strategies, insights from lived experiences, and expert advice to help women with ADHD find focus, fulfillment, and resilience in a world that often fails to recognize their strengths.

Recognizing the unique manifestations of ADHD in women

Understanding ADHD in women requires a nuanced perspective that acknowledges the distinct ways in which the condition manifests in female individuals. While the stereotypical image of ADHD often emphasizes hyperactivity and impulsivity, women with ADHD may present with a diverse array of symptoms that are less overt but equally impactful on their daily lives.

1. Inattentiveness Over Hyperactivity: Unlike their male counterparts who may display more externalized symptoms of hyperactivity, women with ADHD often exhibit greater levels of inattentiveness. They may struggle with maintaining focus, staying organized, and completing tasks, leading to difficulties in academic, professional, and personal spheres.

2. Emotional Dysregulation and Rejection Sensitivity: Many women with ADHD experience heightened emotional sensitivity and difficulty regulating their emotions. They may be more prone to mood swings, impulsivity, and rejection sensitivity, which can significantly impact their relationships and self-esteem. Understanding and managing these emotional challenges are crucial aspects of coping with ADHD for women.

3. Masking and Camouflaging Behaviors: In order to cope with societal expectations and avoid drawing attention to their struggles, women with ADHD often develop masking or camouflaging behaviors. They may expend tremendous energy trying to appear organized, competent, and attentive, even as they grapple with internal chaos and distraction. This masking can lead to feelings of exhaustion, impostor syndrome, and a sense of disconnection from one's authentic self.

4. Executive Functioning Challenges: Executive functioning difficulties, such as poor time management, impulsivity, and trouble with organization, are common hallmarks of ADHD in women. These challenges can manifest in a variety of contexts, from forgetting appointments to struggling with financial management, and may contribute to feelings of overwhelm and frustration.

5. Relationship Dynamics and Social Challenges: The impact of ADHD on women extends beyond individual functioning to affect their interpersonal relationships and social interactions. Women with ADHD may struggle with maintaining friendships, managing family dynamics, and navigating romantic partnerships due to difficulties with communication, emotional regulation, and follow-through.

By recognizing and validating the unique manifestations of ADHD in women, we can foster greater understanding, empathy, and support for women living with this condition. In the subsequent chapters, we will explore practical strategies, interventions, and resources designed to help women harness their strengths, overcome challenges, and cultivate a sense of empowerment and self-acceptance in their journey with ADHD.

The importance of diagnosis and seeking professional support

Accurate diagnosis and expert help are frequently the first crucial steps for women on the road toward understanding and treating ADHD. Even while getting a diagnosis and receiving therapy might be difficult, it is the first step toward self-awareness, empowerment, and practical management techniques.

Understanding the Symptoms and Signs: Identifying the symptoms and indicators that may point to the existence of ADHD is the first step towards getting expert help. Many symptoms, such as trouble focusing, disorganization, forgetfulness, impulsivity, and emotional dysregulation, may affect women. Women may start to comprehend their experiences and speak out for themselves by being aware of these indicators.

Breaking Through Diagnosis Obstacles: Diagnostic hurdles for women with ADHD sometimes include social stigma associated with mental health disorders, gender biases, and a lack of understanding among healthcare practitioners. Many women may also internalize emotions of inferiority or humiliation, which causes them to put off or even forgo getting treatment. In order to get an accurate diagnosis and suitable therapy, it is essential to confront these obstacles and stand up for oneself.

The Function of Medical Experts: In diagnosing and treating women with ADHD, medical experts such as primary care doctors, psychiatrists, psychologists, and therapists are essential. To arrive at an appropriate diagnosis, these specialists may do thorough examinations that include clinical interviews, standardized exams, and collateral information from close friends or family members.

Customized Methods of Treatment: After receiving a diagnosis, women with ADHD may choose from a range of individualized treatment plans. Medication management, counseling, coaching, behavioral interventions, and lifestyle changes are a few examples of these. Through collaboration with skilled and compassionate healthcare practitioners, women may create customized treatment regimens that cater to their specific needs and objectives.

Creating a Network of Support: Developing a solid support network may be crucial to managing the challenges of living with ADHD in addition to receiving professional help. Peer support groups, sympathetic friends, understanding family members, and online forums where women may trade resources, swap stories, and find encouragement and affirmation are examples of this network.

Accepting Autonomy and Self-Determination: Above all, getting help from a professional for ADHD is a powerful and self-advocacy move. Women with ADHD may start a path of self-discovery, development, and resilience by taking charge of their mental health and well-being. Women may embrace their neurodiversity as a source of strength and resilience by embracing their education, engaging in self-care activities, and making a commitment to self-compassion.

We will go into more detail about the many coping mechanisms, lifestyle modifications, and treatment modalities that women with ADHD may use on their way to happiness and well-being in the next chapters. Women with ADHD may flourish and lead meaningful lives that are in line with their beliefs and objectives by adopting a comprehensive approach to self-care and assistance.

Chapter 2: Embracing Your Uniqueness

- **Celebrating the strengths of women with ADHD**
- **Navigating challenges without self-judgment**
- **Building self-compassion and resilience**

Celebrating the strengths of women with ADHD

While ADHD presents its own set of challenges, it is also accompanied by a myriad of strengths and unique qualities that contribute to the rich tapestry of women's experiences. In this chapter, we celebrate the diverse strengths of women with ADHD, recognizing their resilience, creativity, and capacity for innovation in the face of adversity.

1. Creativity and Outside-the-Box Thinking: Women with ADHD often possess remarkable creativity and a penchant for thinking outside the box. Their unconventional perspectives, ability to connect disparate ideas, and flair for improvisation can lead to innovative solutions, groundbreaking ideas, and artistic expressions that enrich the world around them.

2. Hyperfocus and Intense Passion: While difficulties with attention and focus are hallmark symptoms of ADHD, many women also experience periods of hyperfocus—a state of intense concentration and absorption in a task or activity that captivates their interest. Harnessing this hyperfocus, women with ADHD can immerse themselves fully in projects, hobbies, and pursuits that ignite their passion and fuel their sense of purpose.

3. Empathy and Emotional Sensitivity: Women with ADHD often possess heightened empathy and emotional sensitivity, attuned to the feelings and experiences of others in profound ways. Their ability to empathize deeply, offer support, and cultivate meaningful connections can foster nurturing relationships and compassionate communities that thrive on understanding and acceptance.

4. Resilience and Adaptability: Living with ADHD requires resilience and adaptability in the face of uncertainty, setbacks, and unforeseen challenges. Women with ADHD demonstrate remarkable resilience in navigating the complexities of daily life, bouncing back from adversity, and embracing opportunities for growth and self-discovery along the way.

5. Dynamic Multitasking and Versatility: Despite the common perception that ADHD impedes multitasking, many women with ADHD excel in juggling multiple tasks and responsibilities simultaneously. Their dynamic multitasking abilities, coupled with a penchant for versatility and adaptability, allow them to thrive in diverse environments and navigate complex situations with grace and agility.

6. Unbridled Enthusiasm and Energy: Women with ADHD often exude unbridled enthusiasm and infectious energy that can inspire and uplift those around them. Their zest for life, adventurous spirit, and willingness to embrace new experiences infuse every moment with excitement, spontaneity, and possibility.

By celebrating the strengths of women with ADHD, we challenge prevailing narratives of deficit and pathology, affirming their inherent worth, dignity, and potential for greatness. In the chapters that follow, we explore strategies, tools, and resources designed to amplify these strengths, cultivate self-compassion, and foster a sense of belonging and empowerment within the ADHD community. Together, we honor the resilience, creativity, and boundless potential of women with ADHD as they navigate the complexities of life with courage, grace, and unwavering determination.

Navigating challenges without self-judgment

Living with ADHD brings a multitude of challenges, from struggles with focus and organization to difficulties in managing emotions and relationships. In the midst of these challenges, it is all too easy for women with ADHD to succumb to self-judgment, criticism, and feelings of inadequacy. However, cultivating self-compassion and resilience is essential for navigating the ups and downs of life with ADHD.

Embracing Self-Compassion: Self-compassion is the cornerstone of emotional well-being for women with ADHD. It involves treating oneself with kindness, understanding, and acceptance, especially in moments of difficulty or distress. Rather than berating oneself for perceived shortcomings or mistakes, practicing self-compassion allows women with ADHD to respond to their struggles with patience, empathy, and gentleness.

Recognizing Limitations as Opportunities for Growth: Living with ADHD means navigating a unique set of strengths and limitations. Instead of viewing limitations as barriers to success or happiness, women with ADHD can reframe them as opportunities for growth, learning, and self-discovery. By embracing a growth mindset, they can approach challenges with curiosity, resilience, and a willingness to explore new possibilities.

Cultivating Mindfulness and Presence: Mindfulness offers women with ADHD a powerful tool for grounding themselves in the present moment and fostering greater awareness of their thoughts, emotions, and sensations. Through mindfulness practices such as meditation, deep breathing, and body scans, they can cultivate a sense of calm, clarity, and centeredness amidst the chaos of daily life.

Challenging Perfectionism and All-or-Nothing Thinking: Perfectionism and all-or-nothing thinking are common pitfalls for women with ADHD, leading to unrealistic expectations, fear of failure, and chronic self-doubt. By challenging these unhelpful patterns of thinking and embracing imperfection as a natural part of the human experience, women with ADHD can free themselves from the tyranny of perfection and cultivate greater resilience in the face of adversity.

Seeking Support and Connection: Navigating challenges without self-judgment requires the support and understanding of others who share similar experiences. Women with ADHD can seek out support groups, online communities, and peer networks where they can connect with fellow travelers on the journey of self-discovery and growth. Through shared stories, empathy, and validation, they can find solace, strength, and encouragement in the company of others who understand their struggles.

Celebrating Progress, Not Perfection: In the pursuit of personal growth and self-improvement, it is essential for women with ADHD to celebrate progress, no matter how small, and acknowledge their achievements along the way. By shifting the focus from perfection to progress, they can cultivate a sense of pride, resilience, and self-worth in their journey toward greater well-being and fulfillment.

In the chapters that follow, we will explore practical strategies, coping skills, and mindfulness practices designed to help women with ADHD navigate life's challenges with grace, resilience, and self-compassion. By embracing their inherent worth and embracing the journey of self-discovery, women with ADHD can cultivate a sense of empowerment and authenticity that transcends the limitations of any diagnosis or label.

Building self-compassion and resilience

Self-compassion and resilience are essential qualities that empower women with ADHD to navigate life's challenges with grace, courage, and authenticity. In this chapter, we explore practical strategies and mindset shifts to cultivate self-compassion and resilience, fostering inner strength and emotional well-being in the face of adversity.

Practicing Self-Kindness: Self-kindness is the foundation of self-compassion. It involves treating oneself with the same warmth, understanding, and empathy that one would offer to a dear friend facing difficulties. Women with ADHD can practice self-kindness by speaking to themselves with words of encouragement, reassurance, and gentle support, especially during moments of struggle or setback.

Embracing Imperfection: Perfectionism is a common trap for women with ADHD, fueling self-criticism, fear of failure, and chronic stress. Embracing imperfection involves recognizing that mistakes and setbacks are inevitable parts of the human experience and reframing them as opportunities for growth, learning, and self-discovery. By letting go of unrealistic expectations and embracing the messy, imperfect journey of life, women with ADHD can cultivate greater resilience and self-acceptance.

Cultivating Mindfulness: Mindfulness offers women with ADHD a powerful tool for cultivating self-awareness, presence, and emotional regulation. Through mindfulness practices such as meditation, deep breathing, and body scans, they can ground themselves in the present moment, observe their thoughts and emotions with nonjudgmental awareness, and cultivate a sense of calm and clarity amidst the chaos of daily life.

Building a Support Network: Building a strong support network is essential for fostering resilience and emotional well-being. Women with ADHD can seek out understanding friends, family members, support groups, and mental health professionals who offer empathy, validation, and practical support in times of need. By surrounding themselves with caring and supportive individuals, they can draw strength, encouragement, and inspiration from the connections they cultivate.

Developing Coping Strategies: Developing effective coping strategies is key to building resilience in the face of ADHD-related challenges. Women with ADHD can explore a variety of coping techniques, such as time management tools, organizational systems, stress reduction techniques, and boundary-setting skills, to help them navigate the demands of daily life and minimize overwhelm. By proactively addressing their challenges and building a toolkit of coping strategies, they can build resilience and resourcefulness in the face of adversity.

Cultivating Gratitude and Appreciation: Practicing gratitude and appreciation can foster a sense of resilience and well-being, even in the midst of difficulties. Women with ADHD can cultivate gratitude by reflecting on the blessings and positive aspects of their lives, expressing appreciation for the support and. kindness of others, and savoring the simple joys and moments of beauty that enrich their daily experiences. By cultivating an attitude of gratitude, they can shift their focus from scarcity to abundance and cultivate a sense of resilience and inner peace.

In the chapters that follow, we will delve deeper into specific techniques, exercises, and practices for building self-compassion and resilience in the context of ADHD. By embracing these qualities and nurturing their inner strength, women with ADHD can navigate life's challenges with greater ease, confidence, and authenticity, embracing the journey of self-discovery and growth with courage and grace.

Chapter 3: Strategies for Everyday Success

- **Practical tips for time management and organization**
- **Developing effective routines that work for women**
- **Creating ADHD-friendly environments at home and work**

Practical tips for time management and organization

Time management and organization are areas of particular challenge for many women with ADHD. However, with the right strategies and tools, it is possible to enhance productivity, reduce overwhelm, and create a sense of order in daily life. In this chapter, we explore practical tips and techniques for improving time management and organization skills tailored to the unique needs of women with ADHD.

1. Use Visual Aids and Timers: Visual aids such as calendars, planners, and to-do lists can help women with ADHD visualize their tasks and commitments, making it easier to prioritize and plan their time effectively. Additionally, using timers and alarms can help structure tasks and provide gentle reminders to stay on track and avoid procrastination.

2. Break Tasks into Manageable Steps: Breaking tasks into smaller, more manageable steps can make them feel less overwhelming and daunting. Women with ADHD can use techniques such as chunking, where larger tasks are divided into smaller, actionable steps, making it easier to focus and make progress one step at a time.

3. Set Realistic Goals and Prioritize Tasks: Setting realistic goals and priorities is essential for effective time management. Women with

ADHD can identify the most important tasks and allocate time and energy accordingly, focusing on high-priority items while being mindful of their limitations and capacity for productivity.

4. Establish Routines and Rituals: Establishing consistent routines and rituals can provide structure and predictability to daily life, reducing stress and cognitive load. Women with ADHD can create morning and evening routines, set aside specific times for meals, exercise, and relaxation, and establish habits that support their overall well-being and productivity.

5. Use External Supports and Accountability: Seeking external support and accountability can help women with ADHD stay on track with their time management and organization goals. This may involve enlisting the help of family members, friends, or coaches to provide encouragement, feedback, and accountability, or joining support groups or online communities where they can share experiences and resources with others facing similar challenges.

6. Minimize Distractions and Create a Productive Environment: Minimizing distractions and creating a conducive environment for focus and productivity is key for women with ADHD. This may involve setting boundaries with technology, creating designated workspaces free from clutter and distractions, and using tools such as noise-canceling headphones or white noise machines to minimize external stimuli.

7. Practice Self-Compassion and Flexibility: Above all, practicing self-compassion and flexibility is essential when it comes to time management and organization. Women with ADHD may encounter setbacks and challenges along the way, and it's important to approach these moments with kindness, understanding, and a willingness to adapt and try new strategies.

By incorporating these practical tips and techniques into their daily routines, women with ADHD can improve their time management and organization skills, reduce stress and overwhelm, and create a more balanced and fulfilling life. With patience, persistence, and a commitment to self-improvement, they can unlock their full potential and thrive in the face of ADHD-related challenges.

Developing effective routines that work for women

Routines provide structure, predictability, and stability in the lives of women with ADHD. Establishing effective routines tailored to individual needs and preferences can help enhance productivity, reduce stress, and foster a sense of control and well-being. In this chapter, we explore strategies for developing routines that work specifically for women with ADHD.

1. Start Small and Build Gradually: When establishing new routines, it's important for women with ADHD to start small and build gradually. Trying to overhaul entire routines overnight can feel overwhelming and lead to frustration. Instead, focus on introducing small, manageable changes one at a time, allowing for adjustment and adaptation along the way.

2. Identify Priorities and Goals: Before designing routines, it's helpful to identify priorities and goals that align with personal values and aspirations. Women with ADHD can reflect on areas of their lives where they wish to create more structure or achieve specific outcomes, whether it's improving productivity, enhancing self-care practices, or fostering deeper connections with loved ones.

3. Incorporate Flexibility and Adaptability: While routines provide structure, it's important to incorporate flexibility and adaptability to accommodate the unpredictable nature of life with ADHD. Recognize that routines may need to evolve over time in response to changing circumstances, priorities, and preferences. Embrace a mindset of experimentation and exploration, and be open to adjusting routines as needed to better meet individual needs and goals.

4. Break Routines into Manageable Steps: Breaking routines into manageable steps can make them feel more achievable and less overwhelming. Women with ADHD can use visual aids such as checklists, flowcharts, or digital apps to map out the sequence of tasks and activities involved in their routines. Breaking tasks down into smaller, actionable steps can help prevent procrastination and increase motivation to get started.

5. Set Clear Boundaries and Transition Periods: Establishing clear boundaries and transition periods between different activities can help women with ADHD stay focused and organized throughout the day. For example, setting specific times for work, relaxation, and sleep can help create a sense of rhythm and structure. Transition periods can involve brief breaks, mindfulness exercises, or rituals that signal the start or end of a particular activity.

6. Prioritize Self-Care and Well-Being: Self-care is an essential component of effective routines for women with ADHD. Prioritize activities that promote physical health, emotional well-being, and mental clarity, such as exercise, mindfulness practices, adequate sleep, and healthy nutrition. Incorporating self-care rituals into daily routines can help women with ADHD replenish their energy reserves and cultivate resilience in the face of stress and challenges.

7. Seek Support and Accountability: Enlisting support and accountability from trusted friends, family members, or mentors can help women with ADHD stay motivated and committed to their routines. Share goals and progress with supportive individuals who can offer encouragement, feedback, and practical assistance when needed. Consider joining support groups or online communities where members can share experiences, exchange resources, and celebrate successes together.

8. Celebrate Progress and Adjust as Needed: Celebrate progress and achievements along the journey of developing effective routines. Acknowledge the effort and commitment required to establish new habits and recognize the positive impact that routines have on overall well-being and productivity. Be gentle with yourself during times of difficulty or setbacks, and be willing to adjust routines as needed to better align with evolving needs and priorities.

By incorporating these strategies into their lives, women with ADHD can develop effective routines that support their goals, enhance productivity, and promote overall well-being. With patience, persistence, and a commitment to self-improvement, they can cultivate routines that empower them to thrive in the face of ADHD-related challenges, one step at a time.

<u>**Creating ADHD-friendly environments at home and work**</u>

For women with ADHD, creating environments that support focus, productivity, and overall well-being is essential for managing daily challenges and thriving in various aspects of life. In this chapter, we explore practical strategies and adaptations to make both home and work environments more conducive to the unique needs of individuals with ADHD.

1. Simplify and Declutter Spaces: Cluttered environments can be overwhelming and distracting for individuals with ADHD. Simplifying and decluttering living and work spaces can help reduce sensory overload and create a sense of calm and order. Implementing organizational systems such as storage bins, shelves, and labels can make it easier to locate items and maintain a tidy environment.

2. Designate Specific Work Areas: Designating specific work areas at home and in the workplace can help create boundaries between different activities and minimize distractions. Women with ADHD can designate a quiet, clutter-free space for tasks requiring focus and concentration, ensuring that it is equipped with the necessary tools and supplies to support productivity.

3. Use Visual Cues and Reminders: Visual cues and reminders can help women with ADHD stay organized and on track with their tasks and responsibilities. This may involve using color-coded calendars, sticky notes, or visual schedules to provide prompts and reminders for upcoming events, deadlines, and tasks.

4. Establish Consistent Routines: Consistent routines provide structure and predictability, which can be especially beneficial for individuals with ADHD. Establishing morning and evening routines, mealtime schedules, and designated times for work and relaxation can help create a sense of stability and reduce decision fatigue.

5. Break Tasks into Manageable Steps: Breaking tasks into smaller, more manageable steps can make them feel less daunting and overwhelming. Women with ADHD can use techniques such as task lists, checklists, and time-blocking to break down larger projects into actionable steps and prioritize tasks based on urgency and importance.

6. Minimize Distractions: Minimizing distractions is crucial for maintaining focus and productivity in ADHD-friendly environments. This may involve using noise-canceling headphones, setting boundaries with family members or coworkers, and implementing digital tools such as website blockers or focus apps to minimize distractions during work periods.

7. Incorporate Movement and Breaks: Incorporating movement and regular breaks into daily routines can help manage restless energy and improve focus and concentration. Women with ADHD can schedule short breaks for physical activity, stretching, or mindfulness practices to recharge and reset throughout the day.

8. Advocate for Accommodations in the Workplace: In the workplace, advocating for accommodations can help ensure that women with ADHD have the support they need to succeed. This may involve requesting flexible work arrangements, ergonomic accommodations, or additional support from supervisors and colleagues to optimize productivity and job performance.

By implementing these strategies and adaptations, women with ADHD can create environments at home and work that support their unique strengths and challenges, fostering greater focus, productivity, and well-being in their daily lives. With mindfulness, creativity, and a commitment to self-care, they can thrive in environments that honor their neurodiversity and empower them to reach their full potential.

Chapter 4: Nurturing Mental and Emotional Well-Being

- Mindfulness and meditation for managing stress
- Building emotional intelligence
- Strategies for managing mood swings and emotional intensity

Mindfulness and meditation for managing stress

In the fast-paced and demanding world we live in, stress has become a prevalent aspect of daily life, particularly for women managing the challenges of ADHD. Mindfulness and meditation offer powerful techniques for cultivating inner calm, resilience, and emotional well-being in the face of stress. In this chapter, we explore how women with ADHD can harness the benefits of mindfulness and meditation to manage stress and enhance their overall quality of life.

Understanding Mindfulness

Mindfulness is the practice of being fully present and engaged in the present moment, without judgment or attachment to thoughts or emotions. It involves cultivating awareness of one's internal experiences, external surroundings, and bodily sensations with openness, curiosity, and acceptance.

Benefits of Mindfulness for Women with ADHD

For women with ADHD, mindfulness offers a range of benefits for managing stress and improving overall well-being:

1. **Reduced Stress and Anxiety:** Mindfulness practices help women with ADHD cultivate a sense of inner peace

and calm, reducing the physiological and psychological effects of stress and anxiety.

2. **Enhanced Emotional Regulation:** By increasing awareness of their thoughts and emotions, women with ADHD can develop greater emotional regulation skills, allowing them to respond to challenging situations with clarity and composure.

3. **Improved Focus and Attention:** Mindfulness exercises, such as focused breathing or body scans, help sharpen attention and concentration, allowing women with ADHD to sustain focus and productivity in their daily activities.

4. **Increased Self-Compassion and Resilience:** Mindfulness encourages women with ADHD to approach themselves and their experiences with kindness, compassion, and

self-acceptance, fostering resilience in the face of adversity.

Incorporating Mindfulness into Daily Life

There are many ways women with ADHD can incorporate mindfulness into their daily routines:

1. **Mindful Breathing:** Taking a few moments each day to focus on the breath can help anchor attention, calm the mind, and reduce stress and anxiety.

2. **Body Scan Meditation:** Engaging in a body scan meditation involves systematically directing attention to different parts of the body, noticing sensations without judgment or analysis.

3. **Mindful Movement:** Practices such as yoga, tai chi, or walking meditation offer opportunities to cultivate mindfulness

through gentle movement and focused attention on bodily sensations.

4. **Mindful Eating:** Paying attention to the sensory experience of eating, such as the taste, texture, and aroma of food, can enhance enjoyment and satisfaction while promoting mindful eating habits.

Overcoming Challenges and Cultivating Consistency

While the benefits of mindfulness for managing stress are clear, incorporating these practices into daily life can pose challenges, particularly for women with ADHD:

1. **Start Small:** Begin with short, manageable sessions of mindfulness practice, gradually increasing duration and complexity over time.

2. **Be Patient and Persistent:** Like any skill, mindfulness requires patience and persistence. Women with ADHD may find it helpful to approach their practice with a spirit of curiosity and experimentation, acknowledging that progress may unfold gradually.

3. **Create Supportive Environments:** Cultivate environments at home and work that support mindfulness practice, whether through creating dedicated meditation spaces, setting reminders, or seeking support from friends or online communities.

By embracing mindfulness and meditation as tools for managing stress, women with ADHD can cultivate a deeper sense of peace, resilience, and well-being in their lives. Through regular practice and self-compassion, they can harness the transformative power of mindfulness to navigate life's challenges with greater ease, clarity, and grace.

Building emotional intelligence

Emotional intelligence (EI) is a crucial skill set that empowers women with ADHD to navigate the complexities of relationships, manage emotions effectively, and thrive in various aspects of life. In this chapter, we explore the components of emotional intelligence and practical strategies for developing this essential skill set.

Understanding Emotional Intelligence

Emotional intelligence encompasses a range of abilities related to understanding and managing emotions, both in oneself and in others. It involves self-awareness, self-regulation, empathy, social skills, and motivation, all of which contribute to effective communication, interpersonal relationships, and decision-making.

Components of Emotional Intelligence

Self-Awareness: The ability to recognize and understand one's own emotions, thoughts, and behaviors, including strengths, weaknesses, and triggers.

Self-Regulation: The capacity to manage and regulate one's emotions, impulses, and reactions in constructive ways, even in the face of adversity or stress.

Empathy: The ability to perceive and understand the emotions, perspectives, and experiences of others, demonstrating compassion, sensitivity, and understanding in interpersonal interactions.

Social Skills: The aptitude for building and maintaining positive relationships, communicating effectively, resolving conflicts, and collaborating with others toward common goals.

Motivation: The drive and resilience to pursue goals with enthusiasm, persistence, and a sense of purpose, even in the face of obstacles or setbacks.

Strategies for Building Emotional Intelligence

Self-Reflection: Engage in regular self-reflection to deepen self-awareness and understand the underlying emotions, beliefs, and patterns driving your thoughts and behaviors.

Mindfulness Practice: Cultivate mindfulness through meditation, deep breathing, or mindfulness exercises to develop greater awareness of your thoughts, emotions, and bodily sensations, fostering self-regulation and emotional resilience.

Emotion Regulation Techniques: Learn and practice emotion regulation techniques such as deep breathing, progressive muscle relaxation, or cognitive reframing to manage intense emotions and maintain emotional balance in challenging situations.

Active Listening: Develop active listening skills by tuning in to others' verbal and nonverbal cues, demonstrating empathy, and validating their experiences and emotions.

Effective Communication: Enhance communication skills by expressing yourself assertively, actively listening to others, and seeking clarification when needed, fostering open and honest dialogue in interpersonal interactions.

Conflict Resolution: Learn and practice constructive conflict resolution strategies, such as active listening, empathy, compromise, and negotiation, to resolve conflicts peacefully and maintain positive relationships.

Seek Feedback and Support: Solicit feedback from trusted friends, family members, or mentors to gain insights into your emotional strengths and areas for growth, and seek support from professionals or support groups when needed.

Cultivating Compassion and Self-Care

Above all, cultivate compassion and self-care as foundational principles of emotional intelligence. Treat yourself with kindness, understanding, and acceptance, recognizing that emotional growth is a journey marked by progress, setbacks, and continuous learning.

By intentionally cultivating emotional intelligence, women with ADHD can enhance their interpersonal relationships, navigate challenges with greater resilience, and cultivate a deeper sense of self-awareness and fulfillment in their lives. Through consistent practice and a commitment to personal growth, they can harness the transformative power of emotional intelligence to thrive in both personal and professional spheres.

Strategies for managing mood swings and emotional intensity

Mood swings and emotional intensity are common experiences for many women with ADHD, presenting unique challenges in daily life. However, with effective strategies and coping skills, women can learn to manage their emotions more effectively and cultivate emotional balance and resilience. In this chapter, we explore practical techniques for navigating mood swings and emotional intensity.

1. Recognize Triggers and Patterns: Start by identifying the triggers and patterns that contribute to mood swings and emotional intensity. Keep a journal to track your emotions, noting specific situations, thoughts, or events that precede changes in mood. Recognizing patterns can help you anticipate and respond more effectively to emotional fluctuations.

2. Practice Mindfulness and Self-Regulation: Engage in mindfulness practices such as meditation, deep breathing, or body scans to cultivate greater awareness of your thoughts, emotions, and bodily sensations. Mindfulness helps you observe emotions without judgment or attachment, allowing you to respond to them more skillfully and regulate emotional intensity.

3. Develop Coping Strategies: Explore a variety of coping strategies to manage mood swings and emotional intensity. These may include:

- **Grounding Techniques:** Use grounding techniques such as grounding exercises or focusing on sensory experiences (sight, sound, touch, smell, taste) to anchor yourself in the present moment and regulate overwhelming emotions.

- **Progressive Muscle Relaxation:** Practice progressive muscle relaxation to release tension and promote relaxation throughout the body, reducing physical manifestations of stress and emotional intensity.

- **Cognitive Behavioral Techniques:** Challenge negative thought patterns and cognitive distortions that contribute to emotional distress. Use cognitive restructuring techniques to reframe negative thoughts and cultivate more adaptive and balanced perspectives.

4. Establish Healthy Habits: Prioritize self-care and establish healthy habits that support emotional well-being. This may include:

- **Regular Exercise:** Engage in regular physical activity, such as walking, yoga, or dancing, to release endorphins and improve mood regulation.

- **Healthy Sleep Habits:** Maintain a consistent sleep schedule and practice good sleep hygiene to ensure adequate rest and restoration, which is essential for emotional stability.

- **Nutrition:** Eat a balanced diet rich in fruits, vegetables, whole grains, and lean proteins to support overall health and mood regulation.

5. Build a Support Network: Seek support from trusted friends, family members, or mental health professionals who can offer empathy, validation, and practical support during times of emotional distress. Connect with support groups or online communities where you can share experiences, learn from others, and access resources for managing mood swings and emotional intensity.

6. Consider Therapy or Counseling: Consider therapy or counseling to explore underlying issues contributing to mood swings and emotional intensity. Cognitive-behavioral therapy (CBT), dialectical behavior therapy (DBT), and mindfulness-based interventions are effective approaches for developing coping skills, regulating emotions, and enhancing emotional resilience.

7. Be Kind to Yourself: Finally, be kind to yourself as you navigate the ups and downs of managing mood swings and emotional intensity. Recognize that experiencing emotions, even intense ones, is a normal part of the human experience. Practice self-compassion and self-acceptance, acknowledging that you are doing the best you can with the resources and support available to you.

By implementing these strategies and techniques, women with ADHD can develop greater emotional regulation skills, manage mood swings more effectively, and cultivate a greater sense of balance and well-being in their lives. Remember that managing emotions is a journey, and each step you take toward greater self-awareness and emotional resilience is a valuable investment in your overall health and happiness.

Chapter 5: Building Meaningful Connections

- Navigating relationships with family and friends
- Communication strategies for personal and professional relationships
- Cultivating a supportive social network

Navigating relationships with family and friends

The development and upkeep of positive connections with family and friends is crucial for mental health and general well-being. But managing these connections might provide special difficulties for women with ADHD. This chapter delves into methods for cultivating wholesome bonds with close ones while handling the intricacies of ADHD.

1. Communication is Essential: Healthy relationships are built on the basis of effective communication. Tell your loved ones and friends the truth about your experiences with ADHD, including the needs, difficulties, and strengths you've encountered. In order to develop empathy and understanding in your relationships, promote candid communication, attentive listening, and respect for one another.

2. Establish Limits and Control Expectations: To safeguard your time, energy, and wellbeing, set clear boundaries with loved ones and friends. Be willing to set limits as needed, and be upfront and firm in communicating your wants and limitations. It's crucial to control expectations; tell your loved ones about ADHD and assist them in realizing what it's like to live with the disorder.

3. Promote Understanding and Empathy: Inform your loved ones about ADHD and how it affects your life to foster empathy and understanding in your relationships. Assist them in acknowledging your difficulties and confirming your experiences without passing judgment or offering criticism. Encourage receptivity to new ideas and a desire to develop as a team while navigating the nuances of ADHD.

4. Look for Assistance and Linkage: Build a network of sympathetic friends, family, or support groups that can guide you through the difficulties of living with ADHD and provide you with empathetic support as well as practical assistance. Make connections with others who have gone through similar things, get knowledge from their perspectives, and find comfort and support in the support of people who are aware of your challenges.

5. Engage in Empathy and Active Listening: Practice attentive listening and show compassion for your friends and family. Give them your whole attention as you hear their points of view, acknowledge their feelings, and, if necessary, provide assistance and encouragement. Develop empathy and understanding in your interactions to build stronger bonds and respect for one another.

6. Exercise Forgiveness and Patience: Relationship problems may arise from miscommunication, missing deadlines, or forgetfulness while living with ADHD. Together, as you negotiate these problems, practice patience and forgiveness toward both yourself and others. Recognize that everyone is doing their best with the tools and assistance at their disposal, so be kind to yourself and your loved ones.

7. Honor accomplishments and landmarks: Celebrate every accomplishment, no matter how little, with your loved ones and friends. Acknowledge and value the accomplishments of your loved ones, and take the time to show them how much you appreciate their help and understanding. Build a culture of gratitude and optimism in your relationships to strengthen the ties that bind you together.

8. Take Counseling or Family Therapy Into Account: If the tensions or disputes in your family relationships become out of control, you may want to think about getting help from a family therapist or counselor. In order to address underlying problems, enhance communication, and promote more harmony and understanding within the family, family therapy may provide a secure and encouraging setting.

Being a woman with ADHD means that navigating relationships with family and friends calls for tolerance, understanding, and honest communication. By putting these tactics into practice and creating a caring and understanding atmosphere, you may enhance relationships, create stronger links between friends and lovers, and create a rewarding and enriching social support system that helps you get through difficult times in life.

Communication strategies for personal and professional relationships

Positive connections can only be established and sustained via effective communication, both in the personal and professional spheres. Dealing with communication difficulties may be especially difficult for women with ADHD. This chapter looks at doable tactics for improving interpersonal interactions and communication in both personal and professional contexts.

Personal Relationships

Active Listening: Maintaining eye contact, paying close attention to the speaker, and putting your phone away are all examples of active listening. In order to show empathy and confirm comprehension, consider back what you've heard.

Expressing Needs and Boundaries: Let your loved ones know exactly what you need from them, as well as your expectations. Advocate for your own well-being and properly express yourself by using assertive communication tactics.

Empathy and Validation: Even if you disagree with your family and friends, acknowledge and respect their feelings and experiences. Show empathy by expressing your understanding and support for them while also recognizing their sentiments.

Build Your Conflict Resolution Skills: Learn how to resolve conflicts and misunderstandings in a positive way. To settle disputes and preserve wholesome relationships, use problem-solving strategies, compromise, and active listening.

Quality Time and Connection: Prioritize spending time with your loved ones and fostering connections with them. Allocate specific time for deep discussions, cooperative activities, and creating memories with your partner.

<u>**Professional Relationships**</u>

Clear and Concise Communication: In professional situations, it is important to communicate with clarity and conciseness. This means using simple language and steering clear of ambiguity or jargon. Pay attention to your body language and tone of voice to project respect and professionalism.

Active Participation: Engage in active participation in team meetings, conversations, and joint initiatives at work. To show your dedication and importance to the team, share your thoughts, pose questions, and interact with coworkers.

Professional Boundaries: Establishing professional boundaries in the office involves keeping one's distance from gossip and other personal matters that may not be acceptable for a professional setting. You should also respect colleagues' time and space and keep confidentiality.

Efficient Time Management: To be productive at work, meet deadlines, and perform obligations, you must efficiently manage your time. To keep organized and focused on your activities, make use of tools like calendars, to-do lists, and prioritizing approaches.

Collaborating and Seeking Feedback: To pinpoint areas in need of development, get input from mentors, coworkers, and superiors. Work together to accomplish common aims and objectives by using their knowledge and assistance.

Problem-Solving and Conflict Resolution: Approach problems or disputes at work with an eye on finding solutions. To resolve issues and come up with solutions that both parties can agree on, use diplomacy, empathy, and active listening.

Professional Development: To improve your leadership qualities, communication skills, and general efficacy at work, make an investment in continual professional development and skill-building opportunities.

Women with ADHD may build deeper bonds, handle conflict more skillfully, and succeed in a variety of social and professional contexts by putting these communication techniques into practice in their personal and professional interactions. Recall that every connection is a chance for learning and development, and that effective communication is a skill that can be honed over time.

Cultivating a supportive social network

A supportive social network is a cornerstone of emotional well-being and resilience, providing companionship, understanding, and encouragement during life's challenges. For women with ADHD, cultivating such a network can be instrumental in navigating the complexities of daily life and thriving despite the inherent challenges of the condition. In this chapter, we explore strategies for building and nurturing a supportive social network.

1. Identify Supportive Individuals: Start by identifying individuals in your life who are supportive, understanding, and empathetic. These may include family members, close friends, colleagues, mentors, or members of support groups or online communities who share similar experiences with ADHD.

2. Communicate Your Needs: Be open and honest with your support network about your experiences with ADHD, including your strengths, challenges, and needs. Communicate clearly about how they can support you, whether it's providing a listening ear, offering practical assistance, or simply being there for you during difficult times.

3. Participate in Support Groups: Consider joining support groups or online communities specifically for women with ADHD. These groups offer a safe and supportive space to share experiences, exchange advice and resources, and connect with others who understand your struggles firsthand.

4. Foster Reciprocal Relationships: Nurture reciprocal relationships within your social network by offering support, empathy, and encouragement to others in return. Remember that supporting others can be just as fulfilling as receiving support yourself and can deepen the bonds of friendship and camaraderie within your network.

5. Engage in Shared Activities: Participate in shared activities and interests with members of your social network. Whether it's joining a hobby group, attending social events, or participating in community activities, shared experiences help strengthen bonds and foster a sense of belonging and connection.

6. Set Healthy Boundaries: Set healthy boundaries within your social network to protect your time, energy, and well-being. Be assertive in communicating your needs and limitations, and be willing to say no to activities or commitments that may overwhelm or overextend you.

7. Cultivate Diversity: Cultivate a diverse social network that includes individuals from different backgrounds, interests, and perspectives. Embracing diversity enriches your social experiences and exposes you to new ideas, cultures, and ways of thinking.

8. Practice Self-Care: Prioritize self-care within your social network by making time for activities that nourish your mind, body, and spirit. Whether it's practicing mindfulness, engaging in creative pursuits, or spending time in nature, self-care activities help replenish your energy and enhance your overall well-being.

9. Seek Professional Support: If you find it challenging to cultivate a supportive social network, consider seeking support from a mental health professional or therapist. A therapist can provide guidance, encouragement, and practical strategies for building and nurturing meaningful relationships in your life.

Building a supportive social network takes time, effort, and vulnerability, but the rewards are immeasurable. By investing in relationships that uplift and empower you, you create a foundation of strength, resilience, and belonging that sustains you through life's ups and downs. Remember that you are not alone on this journey, and there are people who care about you

and are willing to walk alongside you every step
of the way.

Chapter 6: Education and Career Success

- **Strategies for academic success**
- **Navigating the workplace with ADHD**
- **Advocating for accommodations and understanding your rights**

Strategies for academic success

Women with ADHD may find it difficult to navigate academic obstacles, but with the correct tools and support networks in place, academic achievement is completely possible. This chapter delves into useful tactics and methods designed to support women with ADHD in thriving in educational environments.

1. Recognize Your Learning Preferences: Determine your interests and learning type so that you may adjust your study methods properly. Whether you are a kinesthetic, aural, or visual learner, customizing your study techniques to match your preferred manner can help you retain and understand the subject better.

2. Acquire Proficiency in Time Management: Successful time management is essential for academic achievement. To arrange your time, establish deadlines, and allot time for studying, attending courses, doing projects, and participating in extracurricular activities, use digital applications, planners, or calendars.

3. Divide Work into Doable Units: Divide more complex assignments, like writing research papers or preparing for examinations, into smaller, more doable portions. This method makes it simpler to remain on track and sustain momentum by preventing overwhelm and allowing you to concentrate on one activity at a time.

4. Establish a Study Space Free from Distractions: Reduce outside distractions in your study space to improve concentration and output. Locate a peaceful, well-lit area away from distractions and noise so that you may focus on your studies without being distracted by social media, electronics, or other temptations.

5. Make Use of Active Study Methods: Use active study strategies to enhance understanding and deeper learning. To enhance learning and recall of course information, try out strategies like making flashcards, teaching ideas to others, summarizing notes, and joining study groups.

6. Look for Services for Academic Support: Make use of the academic support programs, such study skills seminars, academic advising, and tutoring, that your school or institution offers. These resources may provide insightful advice, encouragement, and help that is customized to meet your unique needs and educational objectives.

7. Push for Modifications: Don't be afraid to speak up for yourself with your professors or academic advisers if you need adjustments for your ADHD, such as extra time for tests or preferred seating in the classroom. A lot of colleges and universities provide accommodations to help students with ADHD succeed academically.

8. Take Care of Yourself and Manage Your Stress: During times of academic stress, give self-care and stress management first priority in order to preserve general wellbeing. Take part in mindfulness meditation, exercise, get enough sleep, eat a balanced diet, and maintain your energy levels throughout the next school year.

9. Honor Your Accomplishments: As you go through your academic path, acknowledge and celebrate your accomplishments, no matter how minor. Since every step you take ahead puts you closer to your academic objectives, celebrate your victories, recognize your efforts, and feel proud of your accomplishments.

Women with ADHD may overcome obstacles in the classroom, reach their full potential, and succeed academically by putting these methods and approaches into practice. Remember that growth, resiliency, and personal development are just as important components of academic success as grades and accomplishments. Have faith in your skills, endure hardships, and bravely and resolutely embrace the learning and discovery process.

Navigating the workplace with ADHD

Women who want to achieve professional success have particular possibilities and obstacles while navigating the workplace with ADHD. This chapter delves into tactics and methods that support women with ADHD in achieving professional success, efficiently handling obstacles, and realizing their full potential in the workplace.

1. Having an understanding of ADHD at Work: Inform both your employer and yourself about the possible effects of ADHD on productivity and job performance. Encourage candid dialogue and teamwork to build a welcoming and inclusive workplace that meets the requirements of people with ADHD.

2. Making the Most of Your Strengths: Determine your professional assets and skills and make use of them. Women with ADHD often exhibit inventiveness, originality, and unconventional thinking, which may help with project management, strategic planning, and problem-solving.

3. Time management that works: Create efficient time management plans to prioritize your work, establish reasonable objectives, and fulfill deadlines. To manage your workload and set aside time for significant tasks and obligations, use time-blocking strategies, calendars, and to-do lists.

4. Establishing a Friendly Workplace: Establish a setting that will help you work more productively and with less distractions. Organize your workstation to minimize distractions that might impede focus and job completion, such as noise, clutter, and prospective diversions.

5. Divide Work into Doable Steps: Larger jobs or projects should be divided into smaller, more achievable phases to avoid overwhelm and promote progress. Employ strategies like task sequencing and chunking to organize your workflow and keep moving in the direction of your objectives.

6. Looking for Support and Accommodations: Examine the accommodations and support services offered by the employer to assist in managing issues linked to ADHD. This might include adjustments for sensory sensitivity or concentration issues, flexible work schedules, or access to assistive technology.

7. Creating Coping Mechanisms: Create coping mechanisms to control typical ADHD symptoms including forgetfulness, impulsivity, and distractibility. To maintain composure and concentration under pressure, engage in stress management practices, mindfulness, and deep breathing exercises.

8. Standing up for Yourself: In order to improve your performance and well-being, be an advocate for yourself and your requirements at work by being transparent with your supervisor or the HR department about the accommodations and support services you need. Take the initiative to look for resources, clarification, and feedback to help you advance professionally.

9. Establishing a Helpful Network: Create a network of peers, mentors, and coworkers who are understanding of and respectful of your individual problems and talents. Seek out mentoring, networking, and professional development opportunities to build your network and broaden your skill set.

10. Honoring Successes: Honor all of your professional accomplishments, no matter how little. As you manage the difficulties and victories of dealing with ADHD, acknowledge your contributions, acknowledge your growth, and feel proud of your successes.

Women with ADHD may successfully navigate the job with perseverance, confidence, and these methods and approaches. Advocate for your needs, embrace your special abilities and viewpoints, and create a welcoming and inclusive work atmosphere that values and appreciates your contributions as an important team member. In your professional pursuits, you may attain success and contentment if you possess dedication, self-awareness, and a growth-oriented mindset.

Advocating for accommodations and understanding your rights

In order to provide an inclusive and encouraging atmosphere in all spheres of life—including work, school, and daily activities—it is imperative that women with ADHD advocate for accommodations and be aware of their rights. This chapter delves into tactics for successfully arguing for accommodations and comprehending your rights.

Recognizing Your Rights

Understand Your Legal Rights: Become knowledgeable about the rules and legislation that safeguard people with disabilities, such as Section 504 of the Rehabilitation Act and the Americans with Disabilities Act (ADA). These laws prohibit discrimination on the basis of disability and mandate appropriate accommodations in employment and educational environments.

Recognize Your Rights in Education: To guarantee equitable access to education, kids with ADHD are entitled to appropriate adjustments in educational settings. These accommodations might be given in the form of extra time for exams, special seating, help taking notes, or access to assistive technology.

Understand Your Rights at Work: People with ADHD are entitled to reasonable adjustments at work that allow them to carry out their job duties. This might include adjustable work schedules, changes to responsibilities or the workplace, or availability of support services or assistive technology.

Making the Case for Accommodations

Self-Advocacy: Speak up for yourself by stating your demands and any difficulties you're having with ADHD in an assertive and straightforward manner. To bolster your demands for accommodations, include records from medical specialists like physicians or therapists.

Start the discussion: To discuss your unique requirements and look into potential accommodations, start a discussion with relevant parties such as supervisors, instructors, employers, or human resources staff. Go into the discussion with clarity, self-assurance, and a focus on finding answers.

Make Specific Requests: Clearly state what adjustments or changes would help you function at your peak. Be clear about the kind of assistance or modifications you need and how they will improve your chances of success in your career or academic pursuits.

Work Together to Find Solutions: See accommodations as a joint effort including you and the relevant parties. Together, come up with innovative approaches and plans that meet your demands while taking into account the limitations and regulations of the working or educational setting.

Recording Accommodations

Obtain Written Documentation: Make sure that any adjustments or changes that are agreed upon are recorded in writing. This may be done by obtaining a formal accommodation letter from your employer, an Individualized Education Program (IEP), or an official accommodation plan.

Keep Records: Keep accurate records of all correspondence, paperwork, and agreements pertaining to accommodations. For your records, save copies of any emails, letters, floor plans, or other pertinent communication.

Follow Up as Needed: When necessary, take proactive steps to follow up on accommodations to make sure they are carried out correctly and satisfy your requirements. If any changes need to be made, get in quick contact with the right people to handle any issues or make the required changes.

Recognize Your Assets

Seek Advice: Consult disability services agencies, advocacy groups, attorneys, or medical specialists with expertise in ADHD or disability rights for advice and assistance. These materials may be a great source of knowledge, direction, and assistance as you go through the process of requesting accommodations.

Keep Up to speed: Remain up to speed on any modifications, revisions, or advancements to the laws and rules pertaining to disability rights. Maintain ties to pertinent periodicals, websites, and organizations that provide current resources and information on accommodations and rights for people with disabilities.

As a woman with ADHD, you may empower yourself to get the help and resources you need to succeed in personal, professional, and academic situations by speaking up for accommodations and knowing your rights. By means of proficient communication, teamwork, and self-motivation, you may establish a setting that recognizes and provides for your distinct abilities, difficulties, and requirements.

Chapter 7: Balancing Motherhood and ADHD

- **Parenting tips for women with ADHD**
- **Strategies for managing the demands of motherhood**
- **Building a support system for mothers with ADHD**

Parenting tips for women with ADHD

For women with ADHD, parenting brings special rewards and difficulties as they manage their everyday lives and their symptoms while juggling the demands of raising children. In this chapter, we'll look at useful advice and techniques for helping women with ADHD successfully manage the pleasures and difficulties of parenthood.

1. Establish Structure and Routines: For your children's benefit and to help you manage the symptoms of ADHD, establish consistent routines and structure in your everyday life. Establish regular bedtimes, mealtimes, and daily routines that provide you and your kids a feeling of security and predictability.

2. Make use of organizational tools and visual reminders: To help you remain focused and organized while doing your parenting duties and obligations, make use of visual cues and organizing tools. To remember appointments, school events, and domestic duties, utilize calendars, to-do lists, and reminder applications.

3. Divide Work into Doable Steps: To avoid feeling overwhelmed and to make fishing easier, divide parenting duties and obligations into smaller, more doable chunks. To keep yourself motivated and moving forward, concentrate on one activity at a time and acknowledge little accomplishments along the way.

4. Exercise Patience and Active Listening: When speaking with your kids, use patience and attentive listening skills. Give their ideas, emotions, and worries your full attention, and then show them that you understand and are empathetic in your response. As you manage the ups and downs of parenting an ADHD child, have patience with both yourself and your kids.

5. Establish Explicit Guidelines and Limitations: Establish clear guidelines and expectations for conduct, daily schedules, and home regulations. Adhere to these standards with love and respect, and communicate them in a calm and consistent manner. When dealing with misconduct or disputes, use compassion mixed with firmness.

6. Ask for Help and Practice Self-Care: Seek assistance from your spouse, your family, your friends, or ADHD parent support groups. Talk to those who can empathize, validate, and provide useful support about your experiences, difficulties, and accomplishments. Make self-care a priority to refuel and restore your energy so you can handle the rigors of parenthood with resilience and endurance.

7. Accept Adaptability and Flexibility: Accept adaptation and flexibility in your parenting style. Understand that raising a child with ADHD may require unforeseen detours, and be prepared to modify your tactics and standards as necessary. Accept the spontaneity and inventiveness that come with being a parent, and take pleasure in the process of being a parent.

8. Pay attention to connections and quality time: Make connection and quality time with your kids a priority, emphasizing deep conversations and shared experiences. By engaging in things you both like, like reading aloud, playing games, or exploring the outdoors, you may create chances for bonding. Treasure the times when you are with your kid and they help to build a stronger bond.

9. Honor Your Parental Strengths: As a parent of a kid with ADHD, acknowledge your strengths and the special talents and viewpoints you offer to their life. Accept your spontaneity, vigor, and inventiveness as strengths that will enhance your parenting experience and help your kids develop resilience.

10. Put forgiveness and self-compassion into practice: As you negotiate the difficulties and flaws of being a parent with ADHD, remember to be forgiving of yourself and your child. Remember that parenting is a journey of learning and progress for both you and your children, and remember to be kind with yourself when you make errors or don't live up to your expectations. Women with ADHD may manage their own symptoms and overall well being while managing their children's needs by putting these parenting ideas and recommendations into practice. Women with ADHD are capable of being excellent parents and providing a loving, caring home for their children if they are patient, resilient, and show affection.

Strategies for managing the demands of motherhood

For women with ADHD, juggling the duties of parenthood and managing their symptoms may be especially difficult, as they must balance the obligations of providing for their children. This chapter delves into useful tactics and methods that assist mothers with ADHD in meeting the responsibilities of their roles and providing a safe, caring environment for their children.

1. Establish Structure and Routines: To provide yourself and your kids stability and consistency, establish disciplined routines and timetables. To assist manage transitions and lessen turmoil in the home, set regular mealtimes, bedtimes, and daily schedules.

2. Make self-care a priority: Make self-care a priority if you want to keep up your emotional, mental, and physical health. Schedule time for stress-relieving and energy-restoring pursuits including exercise, mindfulness, hobbies, and outdoor time. Never forget that in order for you to properly care for your children, you must first take care of yourself.

3. Divide Work into Doable Steps: Divide duties and obligations into smaller, more doable phases to help with completion and avoid overload. Employ techniques like timers, task lists, and visual signals to help you remain focused and organized while working on the current task.

4. Ask for Help and Support: To help divide up the parenting duties, ask your spouse, family, friends, or support groups for assistance. Assign responsibilities, seek assistance when required, and be open to receiving assistance from others without feeling guilty or embarrassed.

5. Adopt a thoughtful parenting style: By being in the now and paying attention to your kids' needs and feelings, you can practice mindful parenting. Develop open lines of communication, attentive listening skills, and empathy to help parents and children develop solid bonds based on respect, trust, and understanding.

6. Have Reasonable Expectations: Recognize that errors are a necessary part of learning and that perfection is unachievable when setting reasonable goals for both yourself and your kids. When it comes to parenting, be adaptive and flexible. You should be prepared to modify your expectations in accordance with your children's needs and capabilities.

7. Make Use of Encouragement: To promote excellent conduct and celebrate your kids' accomplishments, give them praise and positive reinforcement. Prioritize your accomplishments and growth, and acknowledge even the smallest steps toward gaining self-assurance and respect.

8. Establish Conducive Settings: Establish nurturing surroundings in your house that take into account the individual needs and preferences of your kids. Establish regular norms and limits, set clear expectations, and design areas that encourage self-reliance, discovery, and creativity.

9. Make Self-Compassion a Practice: Develop self-acceptance and self-compassion as you deal with the difficulties of being an ADHD mother. Treat yourself with love and kindness, celebrate your successes and efforts, and understand that you are doing the best you can with the tools and assistance at your disposal.

10. Maintain Communication with Your Kids: Maintain a strong bond with your kids by spending time with them, having deep talks, and taking part in activities and events that you both like. Make time for each other so that you may connect and bond, making enduring memories in the process.

Through the use of these tactics and approaches, mothers with ADHD may successfully handle the responsibilities of parenting and provide a caring and encouraging atmosphere for their family. Keep in mind that being a parent is a journey with ups and downs, and every day brings with it new chances for development, education, and bonding with your kids. Accept the pleasures and difficulties of being a mother with empathy, fortitude, and a wide heart.

Building a support system for mothers with ADHD

Creating a solid support network is essential for moms with ADHD to successfully manage the demands of everyday life and parenthood. In this chapter, we look at ways to build a network of support that offers moms dealing with ADHD empathy, understanding, and helpful advice.

1. Determine Who Can Be of Assistance: Find people in your life who are sympathetic, understanding, and encouraging of your experience as an ADHD mother. Family members, friends, neighbors, medical professionals, and participants in online support groups or communities with comparable experiences might all fall under this category.

2. Attend Support Groups for ADHD: Look for support groups or online forums designed specifically for moms who have ADHD. These communities provide a secure and accepting environment for people to interact with others who recognize the particular difficulties of raising a child with ADHD, share stories, and trade resources and advice.

3. Establish Contact with Other Mothers: Make connections with other moms who may be going through similar struggles in your town or social networks. Participate in parenting courses, playgroups, or neighborhood get-togethers to network with other moms and form bonds based on mutual support and similar experiences.

4. Include Your Family and Spouse: Engage your spouse and family in your support network by being transparent with them about your needs and difficulties as an ADHD mother. Work together to develop ways for handling childcare, parenting, and domestic duties. Encourage them to participate in helping to promote your well-being.

5. Look for Expert Assistance: Seek assistance from medical specialists, family dynamics or ADHD-focused therapists or counselors.

Insights, direction, and coping mechanisms from a professional may help you manage the difficulties of parenting and ADHD more skillfully.

6. Assign Duties and Accountabilities: To ease the burden of parenting and home administration, assign duties and obligations to friends, relatives, or hired assistance. It takes a village to raise a kid, so be prepared to ask for and politely accept assistance when required.

7. Make self-care a priority: Make self-care a priority since it's a vital part of your support network. Schedule time for things like exercise, hobbies, relaxation methods, and alone time that help you feel refreshed and less stressed. Recall that caring for yourself is essential to your wellbeing and your capacity to care for others; it is not selfishness.

8. Go to seminars and workshops on parenting: Participate in parenting courses, workshops, or support groups designed with

ADHD moms in mind. These tools are a great source of knowledge, techniques, and helpful hints for controlling ADHD symptoms, strengthening parenting abilities, and creating positive family dynamics.

9. Honor Your Achievements: No matter how little, acknowledge and celebrate your victories and achievements as an ADHD mother. Celebrate your children's and your own accomplishments, as well as your efforts, growth, and fortitude in overcoming the difficulties of raising an ADHD kid.

10. Remain Informed and Active: By keeping up with frequent correspondence, showing up to social gatherings and support group meetings, and asking for assistance or encouragement when required, you may stay involved and connected to your support network. Build deep connections with others who can support, empathize with, and encourage you as you navigate life as an ADHD mother.

Mothers with ADHD may find understanding, support, and helpful advice to help them deal with the difficulties of parenting with ADHD with grace and perseverance by creating a strong support network. Keep in mind that there are people who love you and are prepared to help you at every turn on your road; you are not alone. Accept the connections and assistance that come from your support network, and allow it to help you succeed as a mother and as a woman dealing with ADHD.

Chapter 8: Cultivating a Fulfilling Life

- **Setting and achieving personal goals**
- **Pursuing hobbies and passions**
- **Creating a fulfilling and balanced life**

Setting and achieving personal goals

For women with ADHD, creating and completing personal objectives is an effective way to concentrate their energies, direct their attention, and fulfill their dreams. This chapter looks at methods and approaches to assist women with ADHD in setting and achieving meaningful objectives, maintaining attention, and succeeding in their endeavors.

1. Consider your priorities and values: Consider your priorities in life, values, and interests first. What is most important to you? What goals do you have in mind? Establishing objectives and values that are clear to you will help you create goals that are true to who you are and will give your life purpose and satisfaction.

2. Establish SMART objectives: Establish objectives that are Time-bound, Specific, Measurable, Achievable, and Relevant (SMART). Divide more ambitious objectives into more doable, smaller tasks, and provide explicit completion dates. SMART objectives give things structure and clarity, which makes it simpler to monitor results and maintain motivation.

3. Concentrate on One Task at a Time: One aim at a time should help you avoid overcommitting. Set priorities for your objectives according to their significance and immediacy, and commit your time and resources to achieving them deliberately. You may avoid overwhelm and improve your chances of success by concentrating on one objective at a time.

4. Formulate an Action Plan: Create a plan of action that outlines the actions and tactics required to accomplish your objectives. Divide each objective into manageable tasks, note any possible roadblocks or difficulties, then come up with creative ways to get around them. A well-defined strategy aids in maintaining organization and concentration as you get closer to your objectives.

5. Make Use of Visual Aids and Memos: Make use of reminders and visual aids to help you stay focused on and aware of your objectives. Make visual calendars, vision boards, or goal trackers to help you visualize your objectives and monitor your progress. To help you remember to frequently work toward your objectives, set up alerts and reminders on your computer or phone.

6. Remain Adaptive and Flexible: Maintain an adaptable and flexible mindset when it comes to creating and achieving goals. Be willing to modify your plans and objectives in response to fresh information, criticism, or evolving conditions. Accept setbacks and failures as chances for improvement and education rather than as justifications to quit up.

7. Honor advancements and landmarks: Celebrate the steps you've taken to reach your objectives and the accomplishments you've reached. Reward yourself when you accomplish significant goals and acknowledge your efforts, no matter how minor. Honoring your accomplishments inspires you to keep pursuing your objectives and encourages good behavior.

8. Take Responsibility: Maintain self-accountability by periodically evaluating your objectives, monitoring your progress, and holding yourself responsible for consistently completing tasks. Think about discussing your objectives with a mentor, family member, or trusted friend who can provide accountability, support, and motivation as you strive to reach them.

9. Make Self-Compassion a Practice: Throughout the goal-setting and attainment process, treat yourself with care and self-compassion. Be kind and gentle with yourself, particularly when you are facing difficulties or facing a setback. Show yourself the same kindness and consideration that you would give a friend going through a similar situation.

10. Take Stock and Make Any Adjustments: Think back on your accomplishments, victories, and difficulties as you work toward your objectives on a regular basis. Evaluate what's working and what may be improved, and be prepared to change your priorities or tactics as necessary. The ability to adapt and continuously develop are essential for achieving goals.

Women with ADHD may develop and accomplish personal objectives that are consistent with their beliefs, ambitions, and skills by putting these methods and approaches into practice. Through dedication, clarity, and concentration, you may take advantage of opportunities, overcome challenges, and build a successful, fulfilling life. Never forget that every step you take toward achieving your goals, no matter how little, will bring you one step closer to your ambitions.

Pursuing hobbies and passions

In addition to being pleasurable, pursuing interests and hobbies is crucial for women with ADHD to develop their creativity, lower their stress levels, and improve their general well-being. This chapter looks at methods and approaches that support women with ADHD in finding, pursuing, and actively participating in interests and passions that make them happy and fulfilled.

1. Consider Your Curiosities and Interests: Consider your passions, curiosity, and the things that make you happy and excited for a while. What pursuits give you a sense of vitality and engagement? Which subjects or pastimes have you always desired to pursue? You might find possible interests to pursue by reflecting about your passions.

2. Test and Investigate: Be willing to try new things and explore a variety of interests and pastimes to find what appeals to you. Take courses or groups, try new things, and expose oneself to a range of hobbies and interests. Accept the process of discovery and give yourself permission to pursue your inquisitiveness.

3. Make a modest, manageable start: When experimenting with new interests or passions, start modest and manageable. Reduce work to manageable chunks and establish reasonable goals for yourself. Instead of aiming for perfection, concentrate on having fun with the process and give yourself space to develop and learn as you go.

4. Welcome Change and Adaptability: Accept diversity and adaptability in your interests and endeavors. Investigate a wide variety of stimulating activities for your body, mind, and soul. Give yourself permission to veer between interests or hobbies in accordance with your inclinations, energy levels, and mood.

5. Schedule Hobbies Time: Despite your hectic existence, prioritize your interests and carve out time for them on your calendar. Allocate specific time slots for engaging in pursuits that make you happy and fulfilled. Consider your hobbies as vital obligations to your health and make time for them in your calendar.

6. Establish a Helpful Environment: Establish a welcoming atmosphere that supports and nurtures your interests and passions. Establish a special area in your house for creative endeavors, assemble the tools and materials you'll need, and surround yourself with supportive and motivating people.

7. Incorporate Presence and Mindfulness: While pursuing your interests and passions, cultivate awareness and presence. Put all of your energy on the task at hand and totally engross yourself in the present. As you immerse yourself in your creative endeavors, give yourself permission to feel pleasure, flow, and a feeling of success.

8. Make Friends with Like-Minded People:
Make connections with others who share your interests and activities. Join social clubs, internet forums, or hobby organizations to connect with others who share your interests in the same things. Being surrounded by encouraging peers offers chances for learning and cooperation as well as inspiration, support, and encouragement.

9. Establish Personal Objectives and Tasks:
To boost your motivation and feeling of accomplishment, create personal objectives and challenges that are connected to your interests and passions. Setting objectives keeps you motivated and focused on your goals, whether they are to learn a new skill, finish a project, or take part in an event or competition.

10. Welcome the Pleasure of Education:
Accept the happiness that comes from learning new things and developing your interests. Take an inquisitive and receptive attitude toward your hobbies, welcoming chances for investigation, testing, and learning. Develop a lifetime passion

of study and creativity to add significant value to your life.

Women with ADHD may enhance their overall well-being and quality of life by embracing their interests and hobbies, which can help them tap into their creativity, curiosity, and enthusiasm for life. Whatever your hobby, it might be writing, dancing, painting, gardening, or anything else, it's a great way to express yourself and develop as a person. Accept the path of introspection and discovery, and let your passions enliven your life and spark your soul.

Creating a fulfilling and balanced life

For women with ADHD, pursuing interests and hobbies is essential to living a happy, balanced life. These pursuits provide chances for pleasure, creativity, and self-expression, all of which enhance general wellbeing and life satisfaction. This chapter looks at methods for identifying, fostering, and incorporating interests and hobbies into everyday life.

1. Examine Your Passions: Investigate your preferences, hobbies, and curiosities first. Think back on pursuits or subjects that make you happy, excited, or fulfilled. Think back to enjoyable prior pursuits and pastimes, and investigate new pursuits that spark your interest.

2. Begin Small and Conduct Trials: Start small and try out a variety of pastimes or pursuits to see what interests you. To discover your interests and preferences, try out a range of events, programs, or experiences. Be willing to go outside of your comfort zone and have an open mind to new experiences.

3. Adopt a playful and creative mindset: Take a fun and creative approach to pursuing your interests and ambitions. Give yourself permission to try new things, fail, and explore without fear of criticism or obligation. Develop an attitude of wonder and curiosity, and approach your activities with an upbeat and daring mindset.

4. Give Consistent Engagement Top Priority: Make time in your daily or weekly schedule for your interests and passions to ensure that you participate in them on a regular basis. View your hobbies as vital forms of self-care that enhance your physical, mental, and spiritual well-being. Despite the responsibilities of everyday life, schedule time for the things that make you happy and fulfilled.

5. Identify Challenges and Goals: To maintain the interest and motivation in your interests and passions, set objectives and challenges. Decide on specific goals or benchmarks to strive toward, such as learning a new skill, finishing an artistic endeavor, or taking part in an event or activity relevant to your pastime. Establishing objectives gives your endeavors focus and direction.

6. Make Friends with Like-Minded People: Make connections with others who share your interests and passions. Join organizations, online forums, or interest groups to connect with others who share your love for similar pursuits. Developing relationships with other enthusiasts opens doors to inspiration, cooperation, and friendship.

7. Establish Specific Areas: Make areas in your house or surroundings that are specifically designated for your interests and activities. Set aside an area in your house for hobbies or artistic endeavors, such as reading, painting, or crafts. Having a dedicated area aids in alerting your brain when it's time to do your favorite things.

8. Acknowledge Presence and Mindfulness: As you partake in your interests and passions, cultivate awareness and presence. Live completely in the present, relishing the feelings and sights connected to your actions. Let go of all concerns and distractions and allow yourself to completely lose yourself in the pleasure and flow of creative creation.

9. Strike a balance between rest and passion: Make sure you get enough sleep and relaxation in addition to your love and excitement for your interests and activities. Acknowledge the role that relaxation and self-care have in preserving general wellbeing. While pursuing your goals, pay attention to your body and mind and respect your desire for relaxation and renewal.

10. Foster Reflection and Gratitude: Develop an attitude of appreciation and introspection while pursuing your interests and ambitions. Take time to acknowledge the happiness, contentment, and personal development that these pursuits provide you. In order to cultivate a deeper feeling of appreciation and significance in your life, reflect on your experiences, lessons learnt, and inspirational situations.

Embracing your interests and hobbies into your life allows you to express yourself and fosters happiness and personal development. Accept the path of inquiry and learning, letting your hobbies and interests add color and depth to your everyday life. Keep in mind that achieving contentment and balance is a lifelong journey, and that every minute you spend following your interests gets you one step closer to living a vibrant, genuine life.

www.ingramcontent.com/pod-product-compliance
Lightning Source LLC
Chambersburg PA
CBHW070759260726
48660CB00005B/1688